D0518374

NATIVE AMERICAN BIOGRAPHIES

THE LIFE OF
GERONIMO

HEATHER MOORE NIVER

New York

Published in 2017 by The Rosen Publishing Group, Inc.
29 East 21st Street, New York, NY 10010

First Edition

Editor: Sarah Machajewski
Book Design: Katelyn Heinle / Sarah Liddell

Library of Congress Cataloging-in-Publication Data

Niver, Heather Moore, author.
 The life of Geronimo / Heather Moore Niver.
    pages cm. — (Native American biographies)
 Includes index.
 ISBN 978-1-5081-4824-1 (pbk.)
 ISBN 978-1-5081-4781-7 (6 pack)
 ISBN 978-1-5081-4816-6 (library binding)
 1. Geronimo, 1829-1909—Juvenile literature. 2. Apache Indians—Kings and rulers—Biography—Juvenile literature. 3. Apache Indians—Wars—Juvenile literature. I. Title.
 E99.A6N55 2016
 979.004'97250092—dc23
 [B]
                    2015031300

Manufactured in the United States of America

CPSIA Compliance Information: Batch #BS16PK: For Further Information contact Rosen Publishing, New York, New York at 1-800-237-9932

CONTENTS

GREAT YAWNING WARRIOR

Geronimo is a famous Native American whose name you may know from stories. However, there's far more to him than movies and legends tell. As an Apache boy, Geronimo was known as Goyathlay, which means "One Who Yawns." He and his father were farmers. He later wrote, "We planted the corn in straight rows, the beans among the corn, and the melons and pumpkins in irregular order over the field."

It was a peaceful time, and the Apache people didn't really have much contact with American settlers. Geronimo learned how to hunt, ride horses, and make his own bows and arrows. He played at being a grown-up warrior. His first meetings with nonnatives were with **surveyors** who were visiting his people's lands.

Geronimo's peaceful childhood was replaced by long years as an Apache warrior. He's pictured here in 1886.

WHO ARE THE APACHES?

THE APACHES ARE NORTH AMERICAN INDIANS WHOSE NAME PROBABLY COMES FROM A SPANISH TRANSLATION OF THE WORD *APACHU*, WHICH MEANS "ENEMY" IN ZUÑI, ANOTHER NORTH AMERICAN INDIAN LANGUAGE. HISTORIANS THINK APACHE ANCESTORS LIVED IN CANADA AND MOVED TO THE AMERICAN SOUTHWEST AROUND AD 1100. TRADITIONALLY, THEIR LANDS ARE CONSIDERED ARIZONA, COLORADO, NEW MEXICO, TEXAS, AND THE MEXICAN STATES OF CHIHUAHUA AND SONORA. THOUGH THEY GREW SOME CROPS, THE APACHE WERE TRADITIONALLY **NOMADS** WHO MOVED AROUND, CAMPING, HUNTING, AND GATHERING FOOD.

A LEGEND IS BORN

In June 1829, Geronimo was born in No-Doyohn Canyon, Mexico. He was a Bedonkohe, which was a band of Chiricahua Apaches. Legends about his life begin with his reputation as a great hunter. One legend says the young warrior swallowed the heart of his first kill to make sure he would always be a successful hunter.

Geronimo became a part of his people's warrior council in 1846, when he was 17 years old. To be accepted, he had to prove he was strong, brave, and smart. He learned all about the tools of war, including religious chants. Great warriors were expected to pray for strength and guidance. During Geronimo's early life, the Apaches fought against the Spanish and the Mexicans who took over and settled on their lands. Geronimo often took part in **raids** in Mexico.

When Geronimo was born, No-Doyohn Canyon was a part of Mexico. Today, it's located along the southeastern border of Arizona and New Mexico.

PEACEFUL AT FIRST

ALTHOUGH HE WAS A GREAT WARRIOR, GERONIMO WAS ALSO A PEACEFUL FAMILY MAN. HE AND HIS FATHER WORKED TOGETHER AS FARMERS, PLANTING CORN, MELONS, AND BEANS. GERONIMO MARRIED AND HAD HIS OWN CHILDREN, AND HE WAS KNOWN TO BE KIND TO THEM. SOMETIMES HE RAIDED NEARBY SETTLEMENTS, BUT GERONIMO DIDN'T START OUT AS THE FIERCE WARRIOR DESCRIBED IN SO MANY STORIES.

GERONIMO WITH HIS FAMILY, CIRCA 1900

A VOICE IN THE WILDERNESS

In 1858, Geronimo went with some of his people to Janos, Mexico, to do some trading. While he was away, Mexican soldiers came to their camp and brutally murdered his mother, wife, and three children. Other women and children of the tribe were killed, too.

After this terrible loss, Geronimo was heartbroken. Some stories say he set his family's belongings on fire, then left to grieve in the wilderness. Legend says Geronimo heard a voice that told him, "No gun can ever kill you. I will take the bullets from the guns of the Mexicans, so they will have nothing but powder. And I will guide your arrows."

In his next battle, he fought with such passion that the Mexicans called out "Geronimo," which might have been a call to the Catholic Saint Jerome for help. After that, he was always known by that name.

Geronimo's life changed after many of his people, including his family, were violently killed. He became leader of the Chiricahua Apaches and led Apache warriors in battles and raids against their enemies.

GERONIMO

DISRUPTION AND CHANGE

No matter what the source was for the voice he heard, Geronimo felt renewed **confidence**. He gathered a group of 200 men to help him hunt down the soldiers who had murdered his family. He and his band of warriors would seek **revenge** against Mexico for the next 10 years.

Around 1850, the United States government had taken over lands that are now the American Southwest. Settlers who moved on to these lands made it clear they wouldn't allow the Apaches to roam in places where there were U.S. ranches, communities, and mines, even though this land first belonged to the Apaches.

Now the Native Americans were limited in where they could live and hunt. Unless they stood up for themselves, their traditional ways of life would change forever.

The United States and Mexico fought in the U.S.-Mexican War from 1846 to 1848, when they signed the Treaty of Guadalupe Hidalgo. Under the treaty, Mexico surrendered land to the United States, including the land where Geronimo's people lived. Once the Americans assumed control of the land, they limited the Apaches' movements and lifestyle.

THE VIOLENCE

SOME PEOPLE GREW TO FEAR GERONIMO, WHILE OTHERS GREW TO RESPECT HIM. THESE FEELINGS WERE TWO VERY DIFFERENT REACTIONS TO GERONIMO'S VIOLENT STYLE OF FIGHTING. HE WAS KNOWN AMONG THE APACHES FOR HIS GREAT DESIRE TO SEEK REVENGE, WHATEVER THE MEANS. GERONIMO KILLED WITH A KNIFE WHEN HE RAN OUT OF ARROWS. HE AND OTHER CHIRICAHUAS WERE KNOWN TO STAB PEOPLE WITH SPEARS, BURN THEIR BODIES, OR SMASH THEIR HEADS IN WITH ROCKS. OF THE VIOLENCE, AN APACHE MAN ONCE SAID, "IT WAS DONE TO THEM...SO THEY DID IT BACK."

INVASION

Shortly after the lands changed ownership, silver, copper, and gold were discovered in present-day New Mexico. Soon, the area was flooded with settlers. They took over Apache lands and treated Apache people with great disrespect. The Apaches fought back. They increased their attacks on settlers. Sometimes they made bloody **ambushes** on the wagons and stagecoaches coming into the area.

The Apache leader at the time, Cochise, was Geronimo's father-in-law. Cochise had spent his life fighting for his people, and he was a respected chief. Now, though, Geronimo and Cochise didn't agree on how to approach this problem. Cochise didn't see a way to fight the settlers. He agreed to the government's offer in 1872 to move his people to a **reservation** because it would mean the end of a long war. Geronimo was deeply disappointed.

COCHISE

After long years of war and raids, Cochise agreed to move his people to a reservation. This statue of Cochise is located at the Fort Bowie Historical Site in Arizona.

TRICKED!

When Cochise died, the government didn't stay true to the agreement it had made with him. Under the agreement, the Apaches were told they would be able to stay on some of their best land. But in the mid-1870s, the government forced the Chiricahua Apaches to go live with other Apaches at the San Carlos Apache Indian Reservation in Arizona.

Geronimo was furious. He felt as if he and his people were imprisoned on the reservation. He and a group escaped to Mexico. They continued to raid and made it very hard for U.S. authorities to catch them. Geronimo wasn't caught until around 1877. He and a small group were tricked into thinking they were attending a meeting that would lead to peace, but it was a trap.

Geronimo led his people off the reservation and into the wilderness. He refused to surrender to the life the U.S. government wanted him to lead.

RESENTING THE RESERVATION

Instead of a discussion about peace between the Apaches and the U.S. government, Geronimo and his band were captured and forced back to the San Carlos reservation.

Geronimo disliked living on the reservation. The people were fed next to nothing and were on the brink of starvation. They were exposed to new sicknesses, such as smallpox. For the next decade, Geronimo and a group of warriors constantly tried to break out of the reservation. They knew the land so well that the U.S. Army had a very difficult time finding them.

Geronimo was great at avoiding capture. Eventually, in 1882, the U.S. Army sent in General George F. Crook, who had been on Geronimo's trail years before. Crook and his men captured Geronimo and his men in January 1884.

TRICKY

GERONIMO HAD SOME IMPRESSIVE SKILLS. FOR EXAMPLE, HE WAS ABLE TO AVOID BATTLE USING SOMETHING APACHES CALLED "POWER"—HE HAD A GOOD SENSE OF WHEN HIS MEN WERE GOING TO BE ATTACKED, WHICH ALLOWED THEM TO MOVE OUT OF HARM'S WAY AND SAVED MANY LIVES. GERONIMO WAS ALSO CONSIDERED A TALENTED HEALER.

GERONIMO

GENERAL GEORGE F. CROOK

Life on the San Carlos reservation was hard. The Apaches were forced to change their nomadic way of life. In this picture, Apache Indians are digging a ditch that would become part of a farming lifestyle that was forced upon them.

ESCAPES!

Geronimo wasn't on the reservation for long. In 1885, he escaped with other Apache men, women, and children who were determined to be free. They hid in caves and canyons. Over the course of a year, the U.S. Army chased an angry Geronimo and his people throughout the American Southwest and the mountains of Mexico. Having returned to raiding and murder, the army began calling Geronimo the "**Renegade** Apache."

But the army was determined to capture Geronimo. They sent **Brigadier General** Nelson A. Miles and 5,000 troops to seize him. That was one-fourth of the whole army! Geronimo and the other Apaches led the troops on a chase through the mountains for thousands of miles.

NELSON A. MILES

The Apaches knew how to live in the mountains and caves of the Southwest, making it hard for the army to find them. Geronimo and his band of warriors are pictured here in the Sierra Madre.

SURRENDER

It was an exhausting chase through the hot summer sun for the Apaches. Life in the mountains was harsh. Finally, in September 1886, a worn-out Geronimo and his group of Apaches surrendered. Geronimo agreed to go peacefully as long as the United States promised to keep the Apaches together. "I will quit the warpath and live at peace hereafter," he said.

The United States once again broke its promise. On September 8, 1886, the United States shipped 400 Apache Indians to Florida. They were packed into just 10 train cars, and many became sick and died. A year later, the nearly starving Apaches were moved to Alabama. Geronimo's new wife Ih-tedda, who was **pregnant**, and their daughter were sent away to New Mexico with other women and children. Geronimo never saw them again.

Geronimo and other Apaches were later moved to Mount Vernon **Barracks** (pictured here) in Alabama.

GERONIMO, THE PRISONER

In 1894, the Apaches, including Geronimo, were moved to live on an army base in Fort Sill, Oklahoma. Life was better there than in Alabama, but Geronimo was a prisoner of war. Army leaders didn't trust him. After all, he had made a life of raiding and murdering. They thought he and his people were using their time to regain strength and go back to this lifestyle.

In Oklahoma, writers came to interview Geronimo. Many asked to see a legendary blanket that the warrior was rumored to have. It was supposedly made of 100 **scalps** of his victims. However, this blanket never existed.

Geronimo pleaded for his people to be moved back to their homeland in the Southwest. The Apaches wouldn't return to Arizona until 1915, and it was under the condition that they live on a reservation.

HUSBAND AND FATHER

GERONIMO HAD MANY WIVES DURING HIS LONG LIFE. APACHE MEN OFTEN HAD MORE THAN ONE WIFE AT A TIME. WHEN HIS WIFE ZI-YEH DIED AFTER A LONG ILLNESS, GERONIMO STEPPED IN AND TOOK CARE OF HIS CHILDREN AND THE HOUSEHOLD CHORES. HE WAS KNOWN FOR BEING VERY KIND AND GENTLE WITH HIS CHILDREN. ONE VISITOR SAW HIM WITH HIS DAUGHTER EVA AND COMMENTED, "NOBODY COULD BE KINDER TO A CHILD THAN HE WAS TO HER."

FORT SILL

Life was a little better for Geronimo and the Apaches in Oklahoma, but they longed to go back to the Southwest.

FAME!

In the late 1800s, Geronimo tried to fit in with white society. He worked again as a farmer, and he also adopted Christianity. By 1898, Geronimo's name was known all over North America. He was even an attraction at the 1904 St. Louis World's Fair.

Geronimo quickly realized he could make money from his fame. "I sold my photographs for twenty-five cents, and was allowed to keep ten cents of this for myself," he wrote. He also made money by simply signing his name.

In 1905, he rode in a parade with Theodore Roosevelt, who at the time was president of the United States. Geronimo met with Roosevelt and begged him to allow the Apaches to return to their homeland, but he was denied.

Geronimo was unhappy in Fort Sill. He longed for the Southwest. He began to drink heavily. He also gambled away a lot of the money he made.

GERONIMO

TELLING HIS OWN STORY

In 1906, Geronimo told his story to author S.S. Barrett, who wrote out his autobiography. It was titled *Geronimo: His Own Story*.

On February 11, 1909, Geronimo was riding home after a day in Lawton, Oklahoma. He had sold some bows and arrows, but then spent his earnings on alcohol. He fell from his horse and landed in a creek, where he spent a long, cold night. He was found in the morning, but he came down with **pneumonia**. He died a few days later. As he lay dying, it's said he whispered, "I never should have surrendered."

Geronimo remains famous to this day. Some describe Geronimo as a hero, while others remember him as a violent renegade. By now you know he was somewhere in between.

Geronimo is known for many things. He was the last Native American to officially surrender to the Americans.

"GERRRONIMOOOOO!"

Maybe you've heard someone shout "Gerrronimooooo!" when they jump into a swimming pool or out of a plane. It turns out that the phrase doesn't have much to do with the legendary Apache chief.

Legend has it that in the 1940s a group from the Parachute Test **Platoon** saw the Paramount Films movie, *Geronimo*. Afterward, a man named Aubrey Eberhardt was trying not to let on that he was nervous about his solo jump the next day. He bragged that he would shout "Gerrronimooooo!" when he jumped. Not to be outdone, every man who jumped after him shouted it, too. It quickly became a tradition among them until the U.S. Army officially decided that they shouldn't yell when they jumped, because it would give away their position to the enemy.

Aubrey Eberhardt's boast that he would yell "Gerrronimooooo!" when he jumped from the plane started a tradition.

TIMELINE OF GERONIMO'S LIFE

JUNE 1829 Goyathalay is born in No-Doyohn Canyon, Mexico.

1846 Geronimo joins his people's warrior council.

 Geronimo's mother, Juana; his wife, Alope; and his three children are killed, as well as other Apache women and children.

1874 Chiricahua Apaches are sent to the San Carlos Apache Indian Reservation.

1876 Geronimo and others flee from the reservation.

 The U.S. government tricks and captures Geronimo, other Apache leaders, and their families. They are sent to live on the San Carlos Apache Indian Reservation. Over the next few years, Geronimo leads his people through several escapes from the reservation.

1885 Geronimo and a group of Apaches escape into the mountains. Geronimo leads the U.S. Army on a year-long chase.

1886 A weary Geronimo reluctantly surrenders. A few days later, Geronimo and other Apaches are sent to Florida.

 Geronimo and almost 300 Native Americans are sent to Fort Sill, Oklahoma.

1904 Geronimo makes an appearance at the World's Fair in St. Louis, Missouri.

1906 Geronimo works with S.S. Barrett to write the story of his life, *Geronimo: His Own Story*.

 Geronimo dies of pneumonia.

GLOSSARY

ambush: A surprise attack.

barracks: A group of buildings used to house large numbers of people.

brigadier general: An officer in the armed services.

confidence: Belief in oneself.

nomad: Someone who is a member of a group that constantly travels with the seasons.

platoon: A small group of soldiers within a larger group.

pneumonia: A sickness that affects the lungs.

pregnant: Carrying a child inside the body.

raid: A sudden attack on an enemy.

renegade: A uncontrollable person who rejects the restraints of law.

reservation: Land set aside by the government for a Native American group or groups to live on.

revenge: The act of harming someone for an injury or wrong they did.

scalp: Thick skin covering the head that is cut or torn from an enemy as a token of victory.

surveyor: A person who studies land and its properties.

INDEX

WEBSITES

Due to the changing nature of Internet links, PowerKids Press has developed an online list of websites related to the subject of this book. This site is updated regularly. Please use this link to access the list: www.powerkidslinks.com/natv/gero